Do You Hear What I Hear?

Parents and Professionals Working Together for Children with Special Needs

Janice Fialka
Karen C. Mikus

A book to be used for self-reflection,
personnel preparation,
and parent-professional trainings.

Foreword by Ann P. Turnbull

Funds for initial development of the material in this book were provided by the W. K. Kellogg Foundation, grant #P0034324.

Printed in the United States of America

Publisher's Cataloging-in-Publication
(Provided by Quality Books, Inc.)

Fifth Printing

Fialka, Janice
    Do you hear what I hear? : parents and
professionals working together for children with
special needs / Janice Fialka and Karen Mikus. --
1 st ed.
    p. cm.
    LCCN: 99-074692
    ISBN: 1-882792-85-8

    1. Exceptional children--Family relationships.
2. Parents of exceptional children. 3. Counselor
and client. 4. Special education--Parent
participation.   I. Fialka, Janice. II. Title

HQ773.7.F53 1999   362.1 '968'08
                              QBI99-1230

DEDICATION

To parents and professionals who teach us that
the only magic to forming partnerships is to slowly,
tenderly, and persistently share our dreams
with each other.

To children with special needs who give us
the reason and opportunity to strengthen our
partnerships with others.

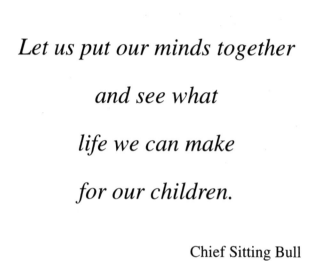

Let us put our minds together

and see what

life we can make

for our children.

Chief Sitting Bull

Table of Contents

FOREWORD

Do You Hear What I hear? Parents and Professionals Working Together for Children with Special Needs is unique. Cutting through the rhetoric and jargon of the partnership literature, Janice Fialka and Karen Mikus offer us an entirely fresh, dynamic, and interactive way to gain new insights. They have "colored outside the lines" in creating a dialogue that enables us, the readers, to gain insights about the partnership dynamics between parents and professionals. In their unique creation, we learn about the feelings, hopes, fears, uncertainties, and expectations from both parent and professional perspectives. Whether you are a parent, professional, or both, you are in for a treat in not only getting more in touch with your own feelings but with the feelings of your significant partner.

Adding insight at the affective level would be a worthy goal in and of itself, however, Karen and Janice take us to another level of insight in also offering suggestions for how we can enhance our contributions—as both parents and professionals—in strengthening partnerships. Thus, I came away from my reading with "next steps" of things that I can do to make partnerships better with the professionals with whom I work. My sense is that you will find the same useful information in helping you take constructive future steps.

Perhaps, the hardest test of all is the "shoe test"—standing in the shoes of another person and seeing the situation from his or her perspective rather than from one's own perspective. As much as anything I have ever read, *Do You Hear What I Hear?* provides an exquisite opportunity not only for taking the shoe test but for passing it with flying colors. I strongly recommend it to you with every confidence that new insights are here for everyone. I'm reminded of Steven Covey's (1990) "fifth habit" which he describes as the most important principle that he has learned in the field of interpersonal relationships. His "fifth habit" is: "Seek first to understand, then to be understood." This book provides the essence of understanding your own and your partner's perspectives.

Ann P. Turnbull, Co-Director
Beach Center for Families and Disability
University of Kansas

Covey, S.R. (1990). *The 7 Habits of Highly Effective People: Powerful Lessons in Personal Change.* New York: Simon & Schuster.

ACKNOWLEDGMENTS

Many parents and professionals have shared with us their stories of becoming partners. We have learned from their honesty, humor, struggles and incredible creativity. We are grateful to each of them and are inspired by their persistence and passion.

We are also grateful to the many people who have reviewed drafts of our manuscript and who offered meaningful and astute comments and heartfelt encouragement. In particular, we thank John Agno, Martha Blue Banning, Lisa Ellis, Rich Feldman, Fran Loose, Linda Klenczar, Cindy Higgins, Ann Turnbull, Vicki Turbiville, Betsy Santelli and Pam Winton.

Our editor for several sections, Carolyn McPherson, had the wisdom to take our reams and reams of written words and whittle them down to the heart and soul of our message. We are grateful for her expertise, bright spirit and strong belief in our work.

Betty Trombetta listened carefully to our thoughts about the phases of partnerships and created imaginative illustrations for each phase. Her drawings brought liveliness to our written words and reminded us that the child is at the center of our partnerships.

Brandy Edmonds, Emma Fialka-Feldman, Micah Fialka-Feldman, Sara Haeffner, and Nicole Samuels enthusiastically created the wonderful drawings that are so important to our book. We are proud and appreciative of their work. They remind us that we all soar when we have meaningful work to do. Thank you to Jeannette Pugliese who orchestrated this art project with her typical warmth and fervor.

A grant from the W. K. Kellogg Foundation and administrative support from the Center for Human Development of William Beaumont Hospital provided us with the rare gift of time to study and to be reflective about parent-professional partnerships. We are particularly grateful to Marvin McKinney of the W. K. Kellogg Foundation and Ernest Krug at the hospital for believing in the importance of promoting more effective alliances between parents and professionals. We cherish this opportunity and know that without this support we would not have had the privilege of learning from so many caring people.

Thank you to Proctor Publications, especially Hazel Proctor, who carefully guided us through the final phases of this project.

Our families are our strongest partners. In so many ways, they have been our first teachers about how to partner—how to form and sustain relationships. Their love and enthusiasm, present even in the wee hours of the dark night, are what nourishes our spirit and fuels our sense of hope.

INTRODUCTION

When we met in 1994, we quickly learned that we shared a passionate desire to understand parent-professional partnerships. From personal and professional experiences we knew that when these partnerships worked well, they were powerful, inspiring and energizing. People on both sides of the partnership felt enjoyment and fulfillment. Children with special needs seemed to receive the most responsive, creative and comprehensive interventions when the partnerships were clicking.

We also knew that when the partnerships between parents and professionals weren't working well, partners felt drained, stiff, and waning in their sense of hope. When this happened, partners said they silently dreaded meetings and often felt awkward and uncomfortable. Too many felt that valuable time was being spent on 'relationship' problems, rather than on planning for and supporting the child with special needs.

For years, we both were hearing that far too many parents and professionals felt stuck in their partnerships—that the partnerships often were more challenging than living with or teaching the child with special needs. These strained relationships baffled us, kept us up late at night and compelled us to study parent-professional partnerships.

We both wanted to understand what skills, perspectives, and attitudes make partnerships work. How is trust developed? How is conflict successfully negotiated? How do you manage relationships when time and resources are limited? We also wanted to know how to encourage, nurture and support positive relationships, especially given the new emphasis on parent-professional partnerships in educational, health, and human service settings.

In 1995, the W. K. Kellogg Foundation awarded the Center for Human Development at William Beaumont Hospital in Michigan, a grant which allowed us the time, energy, and resources to study parent-professional partnerships for one year. We were excited! We conducted a literature review, met with scores of caring, talented, and committed parents and professionals, participated in numerous trainings, and met weekly to discuss our evolving ideas and questions.

One of our final products of this grant was the creation of a full day training on building effective parent-professional partnerships, *The Dance of Partnership: Why Do My Feet Hurt?* We have conducted this training numerous times across Michigan, as well as in Iowa and Indiana. Whenever possible, the training audiences were comprised of both parents and professionals. We believed that it was important for both sets of partners to participate in the same training together—to hear each other talk about perspectives, dreams, worries, and constraints.

The responses from many of the participants at the trainings confirmed what we hoped would happen. Many parents and professionals said that they learned more about "the other side." Many told us that they felt more empathic about the realities and challenges faced by their partners.

As a result of our study of partnerships, our conversations with each other, and the valuable thoughts offered by the participants at our trainings, we decided to compile some of our writings on partnerships. During the year we wrote poems, articles, and snippets of thought stimulated by our conversations and study.

This book, *Do you Hear What I Hear? Parents and Professionals Working Together for Children with Special Needs*, is a collection of some of these writings. In the first section, *The Dance Toward Partnership*, two articles present ways to think about partnerships. In the first article we use the metaphor of "the dance" to illustrate key concepts about this unique working relationship between parents and professionals. In many ways, learning to partner is similar to learning to dance together. Initially, toes get stepped on as partners try to find a common rhythm and shared dance steps. The second article presents a developmental approach to understanding relationships. We have learned that forming partnerships is a process. It is not automatic, but rather evolves over time. This article identifies three phases in moving toward creative partnerships.

The second section, *Beneath the Surface: A Glimpse of Feelings in Early Partnership,* contains the story of a mother who is having her four-year-old Sam evaluated by the school psychologist. The story, offered in six short scenes, is told from two sides of the partnership: the mother's and the professional's. Following each scene is a list of "Ideas to Consider" from both the parent's and the professional's perspectives.

The third section, *You've Got Mail,* explores the benefits and usefulness of "partnership mail." We've learned that when parents and professionals share positive and practical feedback with each other in the form of verbal and written communication, the relationship is enhanced and strengthened.

Our hope is that you, regardless of your status as a parent or professional, will gain a stronger appreciation of your thoughts, worries, feelings, history and insights—as well as those of your partners.

Many perspectives, many voices, and many feelings emerge as we work to love, raise, and teach our children. We believe that when each partner is better able to respect and understand differing points of views, our partnerships will be stronger, more productive, and more rewarding. We also know we will not always agree. We know that each person must feel heard before he or she can begin to negotiate. Therein lies the challenge.

Over the last decade, we as a society have become more sensitive to the harm and hurtfulness of labels. As a society, we are learning that it is more respectful and beneficial for us to speak of the person with special needs, the person who uses a wheelchair or the child with autism. This new format reinforces the individual over the special needs. It is more positive, more hopeful and ultimately more honest.

In a way, we are suggesting that we apply this same perspective to parent-professional partnerships. Maybe it is time for us to soften the labels of "parent" and "professional" and strengthen our ability to see the person behind the role. One way to do this is to take time to listen to our own voice and those of our partners.

Janice Fialka
Karen C. Mikus

June 1999

Section 1:

The Dance Towards Partnership

THE DANCE

Forming partnerships between parents with children of special needs and the professionals who work with them is like learning a new dance. At first the parent-dancer and the professional-dancer do not glide together gracefully across the floor but move awkwardly. Each partner seems to have different hopes, expectations, needs, and constraints. Each seems to be listening to his or her own music, with its own tune, words and rhythm: *The Mother's Song. The Father's Song. The Special Educator's Song. The Therapist's Song. The Physician's Song.* No wonder some dance partnerships are not as graceful as others! The absence of shared music and familiar dance steps causes collisions. Toes—and feelings—get stepped on.

Forming effective partnerships between parents and professionals requires that partners take time to listen to each other's song. This kind of sharing has the potential to open the dancers to a fresh approach and a broader perspective of what the child needs. As parents and professionals share their insights, worries, dreams, and suggestions with each other, a new song is created, one that contains the contributions of many voices. This new song weaves together several perspectives. It's no longer just the cha-cha or the waltz; it's an original musical score with new choreography based on the unique needs of each child.

No one person can "dance the dance" or create the best program for the child. The best plan for the child is built upon the insights, perspectives, and expertise of both parents and professionals. It takes many. Like a square dance, parents and professionals move around the circle by extending a hand to a partner, at the same time holding onto someone else's. The synergy of the dancers creates the most comprehensive and effective interventions for the child.

This dance of partnership is not easy. Partners will not always be graceful and in tune. Few get it right on the first several tries. Master dancers achieve success through practice and skilled coaching. Fred Astaire and Ginger Rogers did not whisk each other across the floor on the first take. They persisted in their practice and listened to each other and their coaches. They frequently stepped on each other's toes and probably felt impatient, bored, and frustrated with the sometimes slow pace. Eventually, they learned to trust each other and to share the same rhythm. Ultimately, theirs was a dance that awed and inspired applauding audiences.

The dance image can be useful to parents and professionals in guiding their understanding of partnerships. To sit at the conference table together and to discuss the child with special needs is an essential beginning, but it does not automatically result in a genuine partnership. We may look like partners but not BE partners—yet!

The dance of partnership results from a strong, ongoing commitment by all partners to listen to each other's music, to try out each other's dance steps, and to feel hope that a new dance will be created, one that integrates the best contributions of each partner.

At the forefront of this work, we must remember that parents and professionals create the music and the dance on behalf of the child. The reward for a well-performed dance of partnership comes from knowing that the child has been given the capacity and support to reach his or her fullest potential. That accomplishment—the evolving and ultimate ability of the child to dance his or her unique dance—is sweet music to everyone's ears!

THE JOURNEY TO CREATIVE PARTNERSHIPS: UNDERSTANDING THE PHASES

We must be partners—now!

There is no escaping it these days. Partnership is a recurrent buzzword in the fields of education, health, and human services. "We must be partners. Collaboration is the name of the game." This is the message of administrators, policy makers, professionals and parents. Articles, posters, and textbooks echo this refrain.

Partnership is indeed a worthy cause, one that appears easy to believe in and own. However, effective partnerships can be elusive, hard to grasp. "So — is *this* a partnership?" "What's it supposed to look like?" "Why is it so hard?"

After reading and thinking about parent-professional partnerships for several years, we realized that some of the frustration felt by parents and professionals working together is due to misunderstandings about the nature and evolution of partnerships. For example, there is often the expectation that parents and professionals immediately are full partners simply by sitting together at a conference table to discuss the plans and goals for a child. Our experience has been just the opposite: that partnerships evolve over time, go through various phases and involve different interactions during various points of working together. This article describes our understanding of the distinct phases which parents and professionals encounter on their journey to forming full and effective partnerships.

It takes time.

Before we explore parent-professional partnerships using this developmental model, it is important to understand the social-cultural context in which these relationships exist. We live in a society seduced by the fast-food mentality. Many of us are used to getting tasks done in very short snippets of time: we have one-hour dry cleaning, one-hour photo processing, the speed of fax machines and e-mail. Drive-in banking, overnight package delivery, and ten-minute oil changes feed our expectations that things can (and should) happen NOW. Right away! This minute or sooner!

But not all processes can be shortened and accelerated. There is virtually no way around the fact that relationships need time. They need to develop through conversations, problem-solving sessions, and overall hard work. All of which can lead to a sense of trust, the foundation of all relationships. There is, in fact, no magic for speeding up the process of forming a solid working partnership.

Nor can we expect smooth sailing and effortless perfection (corollaries of our fast-food perspective). Instead, we would be wise to assume that we will have to work slowly and carefully to become true partners, that we will make mistakes and experience failure along the way, that we will learn to make repairs, and that we will need to use liberal doses of patience, forgiveness, and hope in order to forge effective and durable relationships that benefit our children.

For these reasons, we believe that a developmental approach to partnerships is both realistic and useful. Such an approach suggests to us that there are identifiable phases with tasks that must be completed before partners are able to move to the next level. This way of thinking helps us to view challenges and struggles in the relationships as normal, universal and to be expected, rather than as hopeless indicators of a doomed relationship.

As uncomfortable or painful as some interactions along the way may be, these can often be
understood as part of the process of working
together—toes stepped on in the dance toward
partnership.

Do you want to dance? And other unspoken questions

The dance metaphor is a particularly useful one for understanding partnership. (See *The Dance,* page 3 in this book). But even before two people
get out on the dance floor together, a litany of questions emerges—questions that float, invisible and unspoken, in search of answers that don't
come easily or quickly. It is important to listen for these preliminary questions, however, because they capture the anxiety and hesitancy which natu-
rally frame the dance toward partnership.

Some of the common questions we silently ask sound like these:

• Will you dance with me? Do I want to dance
with you?
• Is this dance floor rough or smooth? What music will we hear this time?
• Which dances will we do? What if I am ready
to dance hard and fast when you want a slow,
gentle waltz? If I follow your lead, where will
you take me? Will you follow my lead sometimes?
• What will happen if I step on your toes? What if
I trip and fall?

And for those who have already been dancing strenuously on behalf of
their children or students, a quiet question, born of exhaustion:

7

- Do I have the energy to learn a new dance? To work with yet another new partner? To keep on dancing?

These are the high frequency questions: not at all unusual, but challenging nonetheless. Ignoring them can complicate the partnership process; being sensitive and open to them can heighten the possibility of a rich beginning.

The First Phase: Colliding and Campaigning

As the questions in the previous section illustrate, most parents and professionals don't know each other very well when they first work together. They typically feel awkward and wary during this first phase. More questions quietly haunt most early conversations: "Who says, what, when and how much should be said?" In some ways, the initial phase is similar to being on a blind date. There is a self-consciousness, an uncertainty, and an absence of trust. Conversations on a first date are often stiff, choppy, and a bit guarded.

Since trust is so fundamental to forming relationships, its absence early on is significant and often results in parents and professionals unintentionally colliding with one another. Their ideas and approaches may seem contradictory and in conflict with one another. As depicted in the colliding graphic, toes are easily and frequently stepped on. Partners seem to be dancing to different music, bumping into each other and dancing in different directions.

In an effort to foster understanding or at least move in the same direction, parents and professionals frequently campaign. Much like politicians during an election, first-phase partners promote their platforms so fervently that they have trouble integrating ideas other than those they originate. As

 the graphic portrays, each campaigner carries his or her own sign with space enough for only one viewpoint. It is the very nature of campaigning to cleverly and powerfully put forward your idea. Dialogue is not part of such an equation.

During this first phase, campaigning often occurs with parents and professionals as they actively articulate their own perspectives in hopes of persuading the other to see the child, the problem or the intervention similarly. In addition, each tries to convince the other to accept the specific solution he or she believes is the right approach. It is not at all unusual for each of the partners, during this phase, to cling to one position because it is rooted in their dreams for the child.

During the initial phase, parents and professionals may not readily listen to each other. People often jockey for power, protect territory, block the other's solutions, and sell a particular position. Although these behaviors seem negative and difficult, such intense campaigning is actually a positive reflection of the partners' strength of commitment to the child or the program. These behaviors also reflect the fact that trust is not readily present early in relationships.

At this point in the dance toward partnership, we frequently hear the language of caution or constraint, including phrases such as:

> "I really want this done this way." "This is the way that works." "That's not how we do things here." "We probably couldn't do that." "My child needs this particular type of program."

Hope and possibility are easily swamped when colliding and campaigning prevail. However, professionals and parents who pause to ask for more information from each other and who try to see the other person's point of view can often find an area of overlap in their visions for the child. They may see points of similarity°in their intervention approaches. Some relationships never really get beyond this first phase of hammering away at separate agendas. If people join together even momentarily to explore possibilities rather than remaining glued to their separate positions, small ways to coordinate or cooperate often surface. Trust begins to emerge, and the dancers are then on the way to the next level on the partnership journey.

The Middle Phase: Coordinating, Cooperating, and Compromising

Partners continue to feel some apprehension and frustration during the middle phase but are also likely to feel more of a balance and some hope. The work is of a more cooperative nature. By coordinating service delivery more carefully at this level, partners avoid duplication and reduce the number of collisions. Partners more often experience each other as being reliable and following through on agreed upon tasks. The small and fragile trust born in the first phase is strengthened when the partners agree to work side by side or to take turns without insisting that "My way is the only way." Compromises can be arranged so that each person feels that crucial goals for the child are being addressed.

At this level, people are more effective in their listening ("Tell me more about what you think.") and more genuine in their consideration of t' other person's hopes, dreams, and ideas. Each feels an emerging sense of respect for the other and begins to believe in the effectiveness of their joint problem-solving. The following graphic for this phase illustrates a sense of moving in a similar direction and of matching each other's steps.

The language which often characterizes middle-phase parents and professionals is the language of polite cooperation:

"You do that part your way and then I'll do the next part my way." "Let's take turns." "Maybe that will work—let's try your idea." "Tell me more about your hopes so that we can include both of our goals."

People are better at asking each other to explain more about their ideas. They are more able to suspend their personal agendas and explore for common ground.

Working together at this level often generates effective programs for children and a sense of satisfaction for partners. Partners' trust in one another and their problem-solving skills can grow to the point that they find themselves climbing toward the third level.

The Third Phase: Collaborating and Creative Partnering

Inquiry and listening continue to be the cornerstones of successful alliances at this level just as they were at the earlier levels. Third-phase partners tend to share their interests, needs, fears, worries, and hopes with one another readily and fairly openly. The security that comes from knowing that your dreams, goals, and concerns are truly important to and valued by your partner enables a kind of exploration and problem-solving that results in brand new solutions—fresh ideas for intervention. No longer are partners dancing separately; nor are there two distinct dance lines as we often see in the middle phase. Instead, the music and the choreography are now original works. Together the partners have written new music and designed new dance steps.

Partners at this third level typically see the child in a similar way and share common dreams for him or her. When situations are viewed differently, which still happens, partners are open to exploring and understanding the differences. As seen in the dance graphic which depicts this third level of creative partnering, the child is central to the dance. He or she is in the middle, the focus, the reason for the partnership.

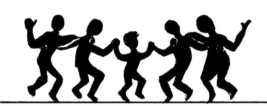

During this phase, partners do not feel the need to have and sell their solutions; rather they believe that innovative and totally new solutions are possible and probable if they join one another instead of taking turns or working alone. When conflict or differences in opinion are present, they are not viewed as threatening. Stomachs don't churn and faces don't flush quite as easily as they do in the earlier phases. Conflict during this phase is acknowledged as a normal part of partnering and viewed as an opportunity to really work on the "important issues" to ensure that the child reaches his or her potential. Partners know that they will get a clearer understanding of everyone's concerns and hopes as they explore the conflict and differing ways of viewing the problem. Challenges still occur. Toes get stepped on. Instead of ignoring or glossing over the injury, however, partners at this level acknowledge their part and offer the necessary "repairs" with care and compassion.

Power and decision-making tend to be balanced. Interventions become blended, integrated, and unique.

The language often heard is the language of creative opportunity and possibility which sounds like:

"Let's see what we can create together." "I think 'ours' is better that 'mine' or 'yours'." "I've been worried about this program for my child. I want to think about it with you so we can create something that will really work for her. What do you think?"

Creative partners experience a sense of excitement and promise as well as feelings of efficacy and satisfaction. Their solutions are far from perfect but can be adjusted and refined in order to assure the best setting, supports, and interventions for the child.

This is the phase in the relationship that genuinely feels good and satisfying.

A Few Caveats

As in all developmental models, no one dances through these three phases in a clear, predictable, and ascending manner. We move up and down, back and forth, get stuck, skip stages, repeat and revisit former phases. Circumstances can cause us to move erratically in our relationships. For example, a new diagnosis, a transition to a new school or program, a change in personnel, and family stressors for either the parents or the professionals can all have an impact on our ability to partner. Each child, family, and team of professionals has a unique way of interacting and finding the way on this journey toward creative partnering. There is no one right path. We have also learned from many parents and professionals that few working relationships get to the third level of creative partnering. Think about it. Most of us have only a few people throughout our lives with whom we can feel that unwavering sense of trust. The third phase of partnership as described here takes time, conversation, courage and a strong belief that working on the relationship is worth it, in the short run and long run.

Each level is purposeful and is rooted in real events and expectations. Our hope is that we gain insight as we better understand our location in these phases. If we know where we are with our partners, then we are more apt to be able to know how we got there and what, if anything, we can do to move forward.

We will not be able to dance gracefully with everyone. Sometimes we have to ask others to do the dancing for us when we encounter someone with whom we feel at a standstill. This type of intervention need not be seen as a failure, but rather as a creative way to deal with personalities that may clash or with circumstances which need more time or a fresh approach.

What seems important to us is that we all pay attention to the relationship and not discount or underestimate its significance in creating and achieving meaningful programs for our children. In our partnership trainings, we suggest that the first goal of every *Individualized Family Services Plan* (IFSP), *Individualized Education Plan* (IEP), or any other service plan be to strengthen the parent-professional partnership. When we suggest this, members of the audience often smile in amusement but begin nodding their heads in agreement: "Yes, that makes sense." When we genuinely function as a team comprised of full partners, then the plan we've mapped out is more attainable. Then the dreams for the child, born out of love and care, are more likely to be fulfilled.

Section 2:

Beneath the Surface:
A Glimpse of Feelings
in Early Partnership

The dance of partnership is an adventure with an array of emotions and reactions that parents and professionals experience along the way. Partners' feelings and thoughts are unique to the people involved but their existence is a reality. All too often, however, these feelings, concerns, and hopes remain unarticulated and unaddressed – hidden voices. The power of unspoken worries and reactions should not be underestimated as they shape relationships and determine outcomes for the children involved.

Therefore, if partners can become more aware of and sensitive to these needs and emotions, some of the stress and misunderstanding generated in partnerships might be reduced. Collaboration on behalf of children could then be that much more effective and enduring.

It is in this spirit that we offer the following descriptions of some of the internal experiences for each partner during a child's assessment. The wondering, doubts, and responses shared by Mrs. Lewis, the mother, and Dr. Gordon, the professional, may be experienced by caring, competent and (even) seasoned parents and professionals every day at all levels of partnership.

The Situation

John and Susan Lewis have one child, Sam, who is four years old. Over the years, Sam has become an engaging and active child who also has developed differently and more slowly than many of his peers. Some of Sam's delays are

worrisome to his parents. John and Susan have taken Sam to several physicians and other professionals who have conducted numerous assessments of Sam's strengths and needs. Most recently, Sam has been referred to the school psychologist, Dr. Rhonda Gordon, for a complete assessment in preparation for a kindergarten placement.

Our Story's Design

These six scenes describe six moments in the lives of John and Susan Lewis, their child, Sam and Dr. Gordon. The scenes take place before, during, and after the initial assessment of Sam by the school psychologist.

Each of the six scenes is presented from two perspectives: the mother's thoughts and feelings are described followed by the professional's. After each scene, two lists of practical suggestions and considerations are offered: one list contains suggestions for professionals to consider from the parent perspective and the second list contains suggestions for the parents to consider from the professional perspective.

SCENE 1

THE PARENT'S VOICE

John, Sam, and I have been ushered into your office. I had no idea there was an additional wing to our neighborhood school. But I never thought my child might need special education services, either. Sam is clutching his pride and joy, his new blue train engine. He sings out "Choo-choo" as you greet us.

Since before his birth, we've had wonderful dreams for our son. We bring you our dreams, our doubts, and our fears. Why is he different? What should we be doing?

We've been through so much in the last two years. First our pediatrician said, "Everything is going to be fine. Sam's just a bit slower. He'll catch up." We tried to believe him, but after a few months and not much "catch up," I took him to another pediatrician. She wasn't as confident that his delays were typical. She led us to a neurologist, a geneticist, an audiologist, a speech therapist, more and more tests, and now to you, the school psychologist. It was hard to pick up the phone to make this appointment— you have no idea how hard. Just filling out your paperwork took more strength than I ever thought I had. Stepping over your threshold was an act of pure will. For us, everything we've wanted and hoped for is on the line. I wonder if you know that.

Our feelings are mixed. I find myself chanting: "Do well . . . don't do well . . . do well . . . don't do well . . . ." Part of me hopes my son will let you see all his difficulties and delays so you can get him more help. Part of me hopes just as hard that you will see all his strengths and abilities—so we won't need any more tests, any more specialists.

Please know this. I'm not sure I can handle one more person telling me my child isn't "normal." I'm scared. At times, my husband and I feel lost, alone. I wish that all this worry would go away so I could go on being Sam's mom, being me.

THE PROFESSIONAL'S VOICE

As you enter my office, I am struck by your faces: your child beaming with pride as he shows me his toy train, and you, Mr. and Mrs. Lewis, your faces stamped with hope, fear, and grief. Week after week, families like yours come to me with their expectations and dreams.

You may not believe this, but this is difficult for me. You want me to fix it. Probably I cannot.

Your questions are complicated. You need answers, and deservedly so. "Exactly what's going on with my child?" you will ask. "Why did this happen?" "What causes this?" "Will he be able to go to regular kindergarten—or high school or college?" "Could he get married?" "What kind of job could he have?" "Which treatment is best?"

I long to give you answers, but often I just don't have all the answers.

Some parents are angry. Some appear withdrawn. Some are easy to talk with, others are more reticent. Some question my expertise—what makes me think I know what is best for their child? I'm wondering which way will you react.

I must ask you questions about your child that may evoke strong feelings in you. Some questions you have already answered to many other specialists. You must be tired of telling your story over and over. I will try to be sensitive to your feelings.

Are you desperate to hear the words "typical," "age-appropriate," and "everything will be fine?" What if I cannot say those words to you? What if the words I say are devastating?

I want to give you answers, but I worry they won't be the ones you want. I want to be helpful, to offer my knowledge, skills, and experiences, but I worry that, at least for now, it won't seem like help.

Some days, I feel very alone in this work.

IDEAS TO CONSIDER FOR SCENE ONE

PARENT TALKS WITH THE PROFESSIONAL:

- I want your help, really I do, but I'd rather not NEED your help. I didn't choose my child's problems. Most days I wish the problems, the meetings, the tests, the worries would just go away. I just want to be—Mom.
- I'm not mad at you. I'm tired and I'm scared.
- I need your kindness.
- Help me know what other parents feel and think when they go through this.
- Please show me that you know this is tough.

PROFESSIONAL TALKS WITH THE PARENT:

- *Coming in to have your child tested must be very hard to do. Each parent comes with unique worries, questions, and knowledge. It helps me to know what would be helpful to you. I want to know your concerns and questions so I can be more sensitive and responsive. If there are important things you want me to know, please tell me. I will respect your thoughts and be careful with them.*
- *Provide me with complete information about your child, including previous evaluations and interventions. Let me know if you agreed or disagreed with the findings.*
- *Let me know the conditions under which you are coming in for this evaluation. Did you choose to get this assessment, or are you feeling pressured by another professional, by the school system or a family member?*

NOTES

SCENE 2

THE PARENT'S VOICE

We sit down on your gray padded chairs. The sunlight behind you blinds my vision of you and your desk, so I push back my chair.

Sam, my Sam, wanders over to your bookshelf. I know he's looking for books about trains and trucks. Should I tell him to sit down? Or is it okay for him to roam? Which looks better in your eyes?

I'm anxious these days. Is this the sixth or seventh test? I've lost count, but I know there have been too many. Testing days make me even more anxious. I'm less sure of myself. I doubt myself more. How much of Sam's problem is my fault? My husband's? These days we argue more. Is that the reason for Sam's differences?

You seem to approve of Sam's roving. Smiling, you ask, "What do you like to read about, Sam?" My shoulders loosen. I relax a bit in my chair.

Now you explain about the tests you'll administer. I get stuck on the word "administer" and only hear bits of the next few sentences. Sam doesn't want to be "administered to." He just wants to play with his train.

"Any questions?" you ask. I wish I were armed with smart, impressive questions, but I just say, "Not yet." We reluctantly rise from our chairs, and you point John and me toward the waiting room. I want desperately to tell you: Sam often needs to have questions repeated several times. Sam likes to play hide-and-seek. Sam hates hard chairs. Sam—

There's so much I want to say. John looks stiff, but he thanks you and asks you how long the testing will take. I glue on my smile and say brightly, "Bye, Sam. See you later!" Sam smiles, waves good-bye, and then goes on playing.

I wonder if you have the answers.

THE PROFESSIONAL'S VOICE

Your child has found my bookshelf and is flipping through the children's books I have collected over the years. I am drawn to him and want to join him in his search for train books, but I see your faces, Mr. and Mrs. Lewis, and instead I decide to address your uncertainties and questions.

I explain the tests I will use, the McCarthy or maybe the preschool version of the Wechsler. Your shoulders stiffen, Mr. Lewis. You, Mrs. Lewis, rise from your chair and walk over to your child. You wrap him in your arms, pulling him ever-so-slightly away from me, as if you are shielding him.

Do I look so terrifying? Do my words—meant to comfort—do the opposite? I recall the first time I met with a family during my graduate internship. I was unprepared for the mother's flood of tears as I relayed the test results about her four-year-old son who was diagnosed with autism. She taught me what no textbook could: how painful and frightening this process can be for parents. I have not forgotten that lesson.

I want you to know that I will look at your child's problems, but I will still see the wonder of him. I know he is special. You help me know just how special when you tell me about his favorite games, what makes him laugh and cry—what you love to do with him as well as what challenges him and your family. I want to know what you see, what only a mom or dad can know.

It is in your faces. You are afraid. You think your dreams for him are not safe with me. I feel some anxiety too. What am I going to see? What am I going to learn about your child that you know and wish were not so?

IDEAS TO CONSIDER FOR SCENE TWO

PARENT TALKS WITH THE PROFESSIONAL:

- I'm a good parent. I want you to know that. Please ask what I think. I know so much about my child—more than anyone else in the world. I may not be able to describe him in the same words you use. Let me know that my words are just fine.

- Some days, evaluations and assessments feel like judgments of me as a parent.

- This is all new to me. Please tell me what to expect from your words, reports, and tests. Sometimes I don't know what the "next steps" will be. I can't always remember all the names of the professionals and tests. You can help by giving me written lists of the professionals' names, roles, and brief descriptions of the tests.

- If you tell me about the strengths of my child as well as his challenges, I'll know you're seeing my whole child.

- Give me a chance to ask questions now and later. I may also need to ask the same questions over and over.

PROFESSIONAL TALKS WITH THE PARENT: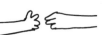

- *Tell me what you hope I'll see about your child.*
- *Feel free to ask questions, now and later. I know this experience might be new for you. Sometimes parents do not feel clear about questions, especially in the beginning. I hope you'll be comfortable enough to share your uncertainties with me—at any point in time.*
- *I try to be careful and sensitive about the words I use. Forgive me if I use some that might offend you or that might not feel quite right. Let me know that, too. I am learning what is comfortable and acceptable for you and your family.*

24

- *One of the tough parts of my work is that I often have tight deadlines and a heavy work load. I will give your child every possible attention.*
- *Please know that I do this work because I want the best for your child.*

 **NOTES**

SCENE 3

THE PARENT'S VOICE

Two hours have passed. Finally, you bring our Sam back. He proudly pushes his train stickers too close to my eyes so I won't miss your gift. I look in your eyes, afraid I might read your mind. I'm relieved you can't read mine. My desperation scares me. You look in control. Why can't I?

You say you enjoyed meeting the three of us. "Sam worked hard," you say. You crouch down to Sam's level and smile. "Thanks, Sam," you say, then add something about meeting us in two weeks to give us the complete report.

Sam's arms and energy pull us into our car. John's jaw is tight. He mutters, "Two weeks . . . . "

Sam bounces in the back seat, kicks the upholstery, and wiggles the door lock switch. He is jabbering incessantly. I try to decipher his words but the sounds are all jumbled up with my thoughts: What did she learn about Sam? Will he catch up? Can we handle this? Is this forever?

Sam screeches his high-pitched squeal, the one that means "You're not listening to me." He's right. He's demanding our attention. Could he get a few extra points on his IQ test for being assertive with us? Isn't this an important sign of intelligence?

That evening nothing goes right. Dinner burns to a smelly crisp, and every credit card company picks that moment to call. I feel so alone. I must visit the funeral home. My friend Linda's mother has died. As I stand in line to express my regrets, I feel Linda's sorrow and loss, but I feel my grief, too. My dreams for Sam are being challenged—some may die. Who will stand in line to console me? Who will even know?

I'm too tired to sleep. I sit up most of the night worrying. Dr. Gordon, what did you find? Two weeks? TWO WEEKS until we know what you think about our Sam?

THE PROFESSIONAL'S VOICE

I am glad we've reached the end of this session. Your child is tired and more than a little cranky. His eyes and tiny body are darting from corner to corner. He resists all my coaxing to get him to play with the blocks. It is time to stop.

He worked hard. I feel my fatigue, too. I offer him stickers, and he pushes through the pile, searching for the right one. Finally, he uncovers a train, of course! He seems delighted with his selection. I am glad. I lightly rub the back of my neck and am reminded how absorbed I become when I test a child. Sam tries to speed down the hall but I slow him down by reaching for his tiny wiggling hand. When we arrive in the waiting room, he rushes to you to show you his stickers.

I smile, but my heart is aching for you. Your child has just demonstrated significant delays in a number of areas, not just in language, not just in problem-solving, but also in motor development and some of the everyday living skills he should have acquired by now. Memory tasks were hard from him, and he could not manage some of the early conceptual reasoning items.

I am glad you brought Sam in for this assessment. I think my findings and your knowledge of your child will help identify some of the next steps and supports so he can reach his potential. But I am well aware that these next steps will feel to you as his parents like climbing a steep mountain in the bitter cold.

I see you greet your child, Mr. and Mrs. Lewis. I know you want me to tell you something, or maybe everything—right now, right this very second. I can't. I need time to think about what I've learned and to prepare a report in a careful and useful manner.

I wonder how much you already realize. I worry that my findings will send arrows through your hearts.

IDEAS TO CONSIDER FOR SCENE THREE

PARENT TALKS WITH THE PROFESSIONAL:

- Waiting for test results is the pits!
- Please prepare me for the challenge of waiting. Tell me some parents feel nervous, irritable, lonely, scared, or sad, that some withdraw for a while, that others feel a burst of energy and attempt to complete every task on their "to do" list. Suggest things I might do to help us through this waiting time.
- I know you need to consider carefully before you can give us results. For now, can you give us an inkling of hope—or some feedback?
- It may be helpful if I'm reminded that I did the right thing by bringing my child in today.
- Tell me you will help me through the next few steps—that you'll make sure we get connected to some helpful resources, other parents, agencies, reading materials. Don't underestimate the importance of these sources.

PROFESSIONAL TALKS WITH THE PARENT:

- *I know waiting is hard. I need time to review the test results and my observations of your child. I don't want to make quick judgments.*
- *If I am forced to delay this process, I will keep you informed and will do my best to complete the report in a timely fashion. I appreciate your understanding.*
- *It may help you to know that I see many families, each with unique needs and desires. Some parents want lots of details; others want the main points and details later, over time. Some parents want to hear every score; others want information about their child with less attention on the scores. There*

is no one procedure that is right for all. If you know what is most comfortable for you, please let me know. I'll try to be sensitive to your wishes.

• *I don't want children to be reduced to test scores. Know that I work to see the strengths and wonder of each child.*

 **NOTES**

SCENE 4

THE PARENT'S VOICE

How did your two weeks turn into three? I tried to be pleasant when the school called to say you had to reschedule—family illness, they said. But I didn't feel pleasant, just upset. This is our verdict. We need to know NOW!

Sam has stayed home with his grandma. As you lead John and me down the long hall to your office, you apologize for the delay and say it must have been hard to wait the extra week. That helps. I want to thank you for understanding, but I don't. It's too hard to juggle all my feelings.

I'm determined to listen, but my eyes fly away from your face to your floor, your walls, your diplomas, your bookcases where Sam gleefully found your books about trains and trucks. You lean towards us, and you start speaking without notes. I force myself to look at you and not the report on your desk. Your voice is direct. You look right into our eyes.

You describe Sam's "charming qualities" and you smile. I like your word "charming." I remember the first time Sam watched "Thomas the Train" on TV. He was munching on his favorite food—homemade french fries with loads of ketchup. He charged right up to the screen to hear the talking train that ROLLED its big eyes. He was so excited he splattered ketchup all over his face and shirt. I almost tell you about the ketchup, but then decide not to.

You fold your hands and consult your report. A torrent of words rushes at John and me, sweeping away my Sam and his ketchup stains. Too many words—they all run together: Cognitiveimpairment motordelayreducedvisualmotorintegrativedyspraxia.

I think, "If I were a good mom I'd hear every word." I must be experiencing a motherhood malfunction. Scored-in-the-fifth-percentile-on-scored-in-the-tenth percentile-on-fourth-percentile-seventh—

The words fly at jet speed right out of my head.

I'm drawn back to your office when splashes hit my clenched fist. I don't want to cry. Not here. NOT NOW!

"You don't have to hear everything today" you say. "It's a lot to handle. We can talk again."

Your words stay with me. I'll replay them later. For the present, John and I search for each other's hands. Silently we ask, "What do we do now?"

THE PROFESSIONAL'S VOICE

I've been worrying about this meeting.

I chose this work because I wanted to make things better for children and their families, not worse. It is heart wrenching to bring "bad news."

I've thought a lot about my report. How to be accurate and clear, gentle and helpful? How to capture on paper your engaging child with his strengths and his difficulties? How to write an insightful, professional report without breaking your hearts?

You both sit so bravely, so straight in your chairs. I begin by telling you that I was delighted to work with your child. "He has wonderful energy and a strong ability to connect with people. I chuckled each time he gleefully shouted, 'Sure!'" Our eyes connect when I describe your child.

Then I move into the more formal findings. My words do not come easily. All the choices seem harsh: Challenged. Compromised. Diminished. Reduced for his age.

The paradox is that to help I must hurt. In order to establish his eligibility for services, I must document his deficits. I worry. Will his strong points, his expressiveness and his persistence, get buried under an avalanche of test scores and terminology?

You both nod, but your eyes look at something far away. I can't tell where you are or what you are hearing. Tears appear in your eyes, Mrs. Lewis, and drop on your blouse and your hand. I hesitate. Do I speak out loud to your tears? I want to reach out and touch you, but I don't know if that would be comfortable for you. What do you want right now? How can I be helpful?

IDEAS TO CONSIDER FOR SCENE FOUR

PARENT TALKS WITH THE PROFESSIONAL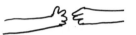

• When you give us initial diagnosis or assessment results, choose a time to talk when all the significant people are available. Let's talk about who I'd like to have present at this meeting.

• Please meet us when and where we can have privacy and no interruptions.

• Refer to my child by name. Tell me what you liked about him. When I sense your regard for him, I can hear your words better.

• Be honest with us. Don't hide what you know.

• Refrain from overwhelming us with volumes of details. Try not to project too far into the future, at least for now.

• Give us examples which keep our hope afloat. We are gradually beginning to form new dreams and expectations.

• Give us as many resources as you can. It's best if you hand us written lists, brochures, and pamphlets to take with us. This may give us direction and hope.

• Be comfortable with our tears, our silence, our frustration, and our fears.

• Don't tell us, "It could be worse." (As one parent said, "It could be better, too.")

• Know that your sensitivity is a great comfort for us. You can't take away our strong feelings, but you can offer support and understanding. Never underestimate the power of listening and caring.

PROFESSIONAL TALKS WITH THE PARENT:

- *I want you to know that I would never intentionally cause you pain or hurt.*

- *Please know that it's normal for you to want all the answers, to know what the future will bring. After all, you are the child's parents. Unfortunately, I do not have all the answers, and the future is impossible to predict accurately. I will be honest with you, even though it may be hard to listen to the uncertainty. I encourage you to ask questions as frequently as you need to.*

- *If you feel unclear about a recommendation, or if you disagree with aspects of the report, let's talk about it. You know your child in hundreds of ways that no one else does: playing choo-choo train on the kitchen floor, dancing at Grandma Rose's party, swinging in your yard, eating his morning oatmeal, squealing in the back seat of the car. Your input is so very important. It helps me create a full and accurate picture of him.*

- *Know that in the real world of qualifying for services, the written report may need to emphasize his difficulties. I will remind you of this harsh reality and will do my best to include his strengths as well.*

- *If you feel I am rushing you through your feelings, please let me know. If I am going too slow, let's talk it over. Our partnership works best when we guide each other.*

- *When you can, give me honest, constructive feedback about this process and my role in it.*

- *Understand that I want to help your child and support you in your efforts in every possible way.*

NOTES

SCENE 5

THE PARENT'S VOICE

It's been twenty-four hours since we sat in your school office, and it feels like a century—a century waiting for news no one wants.

I glance up from my soggy cereal and cold cup of coffee. The calendar on the side of the refrigerator reminds me: it's John's mother's birthday. My stomach knots. It will be the celebration of the decade. How can I possibly drag my body to Rose's party? How can I possibly face red balloons, colored streamers, smiling faces, kids chasing kids? NORMAL kids chasing NORMAL kids? How can John and I walk into that room pretending that we are—just fine, thank you. That Sam is—just fine, thank you. That our future will be—just fine, thank you.

I can picture it now, the voices of my sisters-in-law: "Jennifer is so bright. We're sending her to the Montessori school." "Josh was reading when he was three!" "Courtney's music teacher tells us she has unusual talent—"

No one ever asks about Sam. They know something's not quite right, and it makes them awkward. Tonight we will stand in that room full of kind, well-meaning people, and no one will know what to say.

Dr. Gordon, it was hard to hear what you told us, but it was also a great relief to be able to talk with you. You don't know how lonely it's been, how worried I've been about Sam's delays, how alarmed I've been by his halting speech, how crushed I've been to see his sweet legs fail at running as fast as the other kids.

You had words and explanations for things I noticed in Sam a long time ago. Some of your words felt like new keys to locked doors. I stuck the papers you gave us—the "additional resources for families"—in the piles on my bedside stand. I can't read them yet. Maybe not even next week.

But I will . . . when I'm ready.

36

THE PROFESSIONAL'S VOICE

When I left my office yesterday evening, I was weighed down with loss and sadness. Those feelings lurk just around the corner today and appear unexpectedly while I am at the grocery store.

Two young mothers who obviously know each other are standing in the produce section. Their sons—about Sam's age—are chattering away. I move closer. One of the boys tells a terrible joke—one of those jokes only funny to five-year-olds, and the boys laugh raucously. Your child, I realize with sadness, would probably not understand such a joke.

The mothers' words float across the grapes and broccoli: "Mrs. Miller is a WONDERFUL kindergarten teacher... most of her kids are reading by the end of the year ... and she really challenges kids in science and math, too! When Amanda had her, Mrs. Miller had them all building volcanoes!"

Could your child hold his own in such a class? Would such a setting welcome him? Could Mrs. Miller meet your child's needs, too? Sighing, I push my cart towards the deli section.

Mr. and Mrs. Lewis, you are at the beginning of a long journey. Yours is a trip with no road map and no end in sight. Will you be able to be realistic about your child, about his abilities and his difficulties? You see a child who has more capabilities than I saw—but, of course, you know him better than I do. Or, as the jargon goes, are you in denial? Is being in denial such a bad thing? Could it be necessary? Might it even be helpful? Maybe "denial" means you have the 'pause button' pushed so you can slow down this process and absorb it bit by bit, frame by frame.

I wonder how you are feeling today. Are you prepared for heart-breaking reminders of your son's difficulties—even in the produce department? Will you still be able to see Sam's many gifts?

IDEAS TO CONSIDER FOR SCENE FIVE

PARENT TALKS WITH THE PROFESSIONAL:

• Please know there is more to my life than having a child with special needs, but right now I'm having a hard time thinking about anything else. I feel consumed by this. Life feels fragile.

• I might not be able to follow up immediately on your suggestions. It's not because I don't care or I'm "in denial." I need time and support to absorb all of this—to rearrange my dreams.

• Let me know if you learn about other resources, parent groups, or information that might be relevant to my search for understanding my child and what he needs.

• If you can phone me to see how I'm doing, it may help me feel less alone. I'm learning that many family members and friends may not know how to reach out to me during this challenging time. They worry that they may be intrusive. You, more than most people, have a sense of what I'm dealing with.

PROFESSIONAL TALKS WITH THE PARENT: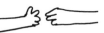

• *I really care about the children I meet. I want to be helpful to them and their families.*

• *If there is something that I've done that was useful, feel free to let me know about it. I can learn from your ideas and feedback.*

• *If something does not work, I want to know that, too. If any of the resources or referrals weren't useful or no longer existed, please consider passing on that information to me.*

• *My thoughts of your child and you, too, do not end when the test report is locked in my office. I like hearing how your child is doing.*

NOTES

SCENE 6

THE PARENT'S VOICE
Six months later

I linger outside the door to Sam's kindergarten classroom. It's my monthly afternoon to be a parent volunteer in his class. Before entering the room, I pause and sneak a glance at Sam through the tiny window in the closed door. I want to see how—or if—he interacts with the other kids. I want to know how he's doing in this "regular kindergarten with special supports for Sam." As I lean closer to the window glass, I'm surprised to see you, Dr. Gordon. You and Sam are digging in the sand table near the corner of the room. I can't make out your words, but I can tell you are trying to make Sam laugh. He does!

It's been months since you tested Sam. Queasiness in my stomach returns, reminding me of those earlier days in your office when John and I sat on those gray chairs near the bookshelf. We were hoping you would tell us, IN NO UNCERTAIN TERMS, that Sam would be just fine. That didn't happen.

My whole world turned upside down that day, but I am still standing. In many ways, I feel different from that mother who sat in your office listening to you use unfamiliar words that scarred my soul. I have learned so much about Sam and the world of special needs. I know about resources, and I am involved in getting the best services for Sam and our family. I've talked with two other moms who have children with special needs. These moms helped me to feel less alone and unsure of myself. They've introduced me to so many resources. I still have many worries about Sam. Some nights I wake up in a cold sweat. Sometimes, when I'm swinging Sam in the park, tears unexpectedly slide down my cheeks. But I also feel a renewed sense of myself. I feel a bit more confident—more determined. New dreams for Sam and our family are beginning to take shape.

Those first meetings with you were so hard. I didn't want to hear your words, yet I knew I had to listen. I remember that you called a week or two after giving us the results of his assessment. Your call and concern meant so much to us. You couldn't make Sam "catch up," but you did help ease some of the worry and sadness. You took your time in answering my questions. You even helped us know what questions to ask. You led us to some helpful resources and other parent groups.

The school bell rings, and I jump. It's time to go in. I open the door, greet Sam's teacher, and walk across the room. I decide to join you and Sam at the sand box. Sam screeches with delight when he sees me. We embrace and then shove our hands into the cold, wet sand. I touch Sam's pudgy, low-muscle tone fingers and wonder what we will build.

THE PROFESSIONAL'S VOICE
Six months later

Whenever I have a minute, I like to slip into the classroom and visit one of the children I've tested. Today, I am spending time with your child when you appear in his classroom. It is good to see you both.

Sam sparkles with his special exuberance for people. He is very sensitive to others. Today, Shauna was longingly watching the other children at the sand table. They didn't pay attention to her, but your Sam called out cheerfully, "Shauna, Shauna, here!" and

he handed her a shovel. It was just the invitation she needed.

Sam seems to be doing well in this class. Mrs. Katz has carefully adapted the kindergarten curriculum for your child so that he is both challenged and supported. I cannot help but wonder if next year's teacher will be as skilled in including him—and the next year's teacher and the one after that? What lies ahead for him and you?

Mrs. Lewis, what is it like for you to work in this classroom where you see how much some of the children Sam's age can do? You look more "settled" today than the last time we met. But I would guess that pain and loss can be easily triggered for you, probably when you least expect them.

I want to stay longer, but I have more than a handful of children waiting to be evaluated. In my heart, I know there will be other wonderful children with loving parents with whom I must share difficult news.

Section 3:

You've Got Mail!

YOU'VE GOT MAIL: MESSAGES WHICH STRENGTHEN PARTNERSHIPS

Communication is the cornerstone of partnerships that work. Communication between parents and professionals, between home and school, or between family and therapist can take a number of forms. For example, parents and professionals, especially in early childhood and elementary school settings, often send brief notes back and forth as a way to update each other about the child's successes, struggles, and unexpected circumstances.

> "Sam had a great day in school. The new dosage of his medication seems to be working well for him."
>
> "Jayne may be a bit distracted at school today. Her sister was ill during the night, so Jayne didn't get much sleep."
>
> "Michael could use a bit more help on his math homework. He's struggling with the concept of subtraction. Thanks so much."

There's another type of communication that we believe is equally important to strengthening the working relationship. It is the feedback offered between parents and professionals about their work as team members. It is on a more personal level, offered by one partner to another about his or her involvement, contributions, or support.

> "Thanks for sending my son the extra math homework. I appreciate your following through on our ideas."

> "It was so thoughtful of you to find the computer program on the solar system. It's really been helpful. Your daughter is having a great time with it and has enjoyed sharing it with her classmates."

> "I wanted to thank you for taking time to listen to my worries about

45

Shaundra yesterday. I know I'll get through this difficult time. It helps to be able to talk about it with someone who knows the situation."

Today we are fortunate to have many avenues for communicating with partners even when we are not face-to-face with one another. Technology brings us e-mail and voice mail. Children's backpacks can be handy communication conduits and the post office still sells stamps for those old-fashioned handwritten notes. Everyone likes to find a cheerful card amidst the bills in their mailbox or some words of appreciation in a string of e-mails.

Why send partnership mail?

Working and living with children who have special needs have powerful rewards but it's also challenging work that demands the use of our hearts, minds, and souls on a daily basis. When parents and professionals receive honest and caring positive feedback from each other, it nourishes our commitment, informs us about what is helpful and just plain feels good. Concrete feedback quiets the unresolved doubts ("Did I do this well?" "Was this ok to say?") and provides some reassurance and confidence that the work is moving in the right direction for the child, the school and the home.

One of the authors recalls sending a brief note to her son's kindergarten teacher telling her how much he seemed to be enjoying music class. "He's constantly singing, 'John Jacob Jingle Hammer Schmidt. . .That's my name too' as he dances through the house." The teacher later said that she smiled as she read the note and was delighted to receive this reassuring feedback. She had been troubled by his quiet demeanor and his lack of eye contact during class. This brief communication strengthened the teacher's understanding of the child and encouraged her to continue her efforts to engage him.

Partnership mail can strengthen working alliances by helping the players learn more about each other's music and dance steps. By letting partners know about their dreams, partner-to-partner mail helps parents and professionals feel 'heard.' By surfacing one's own hopes and concerns in caring messages, partners can make their visions for their child or program more visible and more alive.

When to send partnership mail?

The beginning of a relationship is an excellent time to send a note of welcome. Recently, the mother and father of a young boy with autism approached the end-of-the-year meeting with their son's school with apprehension. The past school year had been a difficult one and his parents were concerned about next year's experience. They met next year's teacher at this meeting and were delighted to receive the following note in the mail shortly afterward:

> Dear Mr. and Mrs. S.,
> I enjoyed meeting with both of you yesterday at David's IEPC. It is clear that he has two wonderful parents who are working hard to help him grow and develop! I look forward to our partnership next year, and I am excited about having David in my classroom—he's a neat kid with lots of potential! Call anytime with questions or concerns, etc.—my home number is 992-8210.
> Linda E.

David's parents are now approaching next Fall with a renewed sense of hope.

Another mother shared a poem she'd written about her son with his new fourth grade teacher. The mother felt a bit anxious and worried as to how the teacher might receive this. The mother felt relieved and reassured when she received an unexpected note from the teacher:

> Dear Ms. P.,
>
> I was touched by your poem and even shed a few tears. I'm glad you helped me understand your feelings. He's fortunate to have you to support his learning and growth. Thanks so much for sharing it with me.
>
> Judy Z.

Mail can be sent after a formal parent-professional meeting (such as a special education meeting or a parent-teacher conference) or after an informal exchange. Messages can also be meaningful when one member of the team is experiencing stress or a difficult time and the other partner recognizes this in a communication. When someone has made a positive contribution or a real effort to be helpful, a quick note of appreciation helps the receiving partner feel valued. For example, this is the note that one father sent to his daughter's teacher:

> Dear Mrs. J.,
>
> Thank you so much for showing Samantha and me around your classroom so she could get a little used to her new room and new teacher. I know that the end of August, right before school, is a very hectic time for teachers. We certainly appreciate your generosity in giving some of your time to us when we dropped in last Tuesday. We're looking forward to Samantha being in your program this next school year. Please let us know if there is any way that Samantha's mom and I can be of help to you.
>
> Sincerely,
>
> Jack W.

Feedback messages are also important in helping partners know what's working and what's not. For example, one mother left this message on her daughter's teacher's voice mail at school:

> Hello, Mrs. Engle. This is Mrs. Harvey, Emily's mom. I know that Emily has been having a hard time understanding some of the details of the solar system. You've been so patient and have really helped to break down the concepts for her. I wanted you to know that last night during a family walk, she was so excited to find the moon. She got all of us to look up and gaze at its wonder. Thanks!

We all encounter challenges as we try to collaborate with others. Partnership mail can be quite useful when partners' visions differ or when conflict and disagreement arise. Toes—and feelings—get stepped on as we dance together. Messages which acknowledge the difficulties and address the feelings can be particularly helpful. Such notes of repair can help heal wounds in a relationship which might otherwise fester and interfere with creative partnering.

One mother sent the following "repair note" via e-mail to her child's teacher after she had been particularly heated in expressing her frustration with the school in a meeting:

> Hello, Mrs. N.,
>
> Thank you for listening so carefully and patiently to my frustrations about Courtney's difficulties in gym and at lunch. I do very much want the school to help her learn to manage these times. After the meeting my husband and I talked about a few ways that we can support your ideas at home and in the neighborhood. Thanks for staying as calm as you did during the meeting. I really appreciate your interest in Courtney. I want to continue to

work with you on this challenging area.

Thanks,

Courtney's mom

Partnership mail, as exemplified in the previous notes and e-mails, helps to make the unspoken thoughts between partners more visible. This type of communication has the potential to give depth to the working relationships that evolve between parents and professionals.

What are some guidelines for partnership mail?

The following are a few helpful hints for composing messages that will promote collaboration and foster the development of strong, effective partnerships.

- Be genuine and authentic.
- Identify the positive contributions your partner has made or is making. Identify the positive aspects of your work together.
- Express thanks for or recognition of the things your partner did or said that were helpful.
- Convey your thanks for the things your partner did NOT do or did NOT say that you valued. Be clear about why the absence of these behaviors was helpful.
- Mention behaviors that you would like to see more of; describe what your partner said or did and how you felt about it.
- Reframe the other person's difficult behaviors. For example, if the partner was demanding in a meeting, you might write or say something such as: "You felt strongly about this idea. You are a strong advocate for your child. I admire that quality in you."
- Take responsibility for your role in a difficult or tense interaction and apologize if that is appropriate.
- Include a statement or two about your hopes for the partnership for the

future. Invite your partner to share his or her dreams and concerns.

- Remember to acknowledge feelings, stresses and efforts.

What are some of the things we have learned about partnership mail?

Over time, our experience with partnership mail has led to several observation. Although this kind of communication is important and meaningful, the recipients of partnership mail do not always respond or acknowledge the messages they have received. This may leave the sender with a bit of uncertainty or disappointment; therefore, it is important for senders to remember that many people treasure —and even save—the handwritten notes, e-mails, and messages they receive even when they don't tell the sender how much the message meant to them.

Partnership mail need not be lengthy or time-consuming: a little thought, a few words of care or gratitude, and a lick of a stamp or press of the "send" button on the computer are all it takes. The return on your investment in this kind of communication may be subtle and may take some time. Be assured that positive partnership mail builds trust and goodwill. It can set the tone for an entire partnership, can nurture every relationship, and can help mend a working alliance that has been challenged by differing perspectives. The care and concern conveyed will be remembered for a very long time.

RESOURCES

This is a selection of books authored by parents who have a child with special needs. Through their honest and poignant stories we can enhance our understanding of the challenges, joys and achievements experienced by families.

Bernstein, J. (1988). *Loving Rachel: A family's journey from grief.* Pittsburgh: Coyne and Chenoweth. (Available only through the publisher: PO Box 8195, Pittsburgh, PA 15127. Phone: 412-321-4587.)

Berube, M. (1996). *Life as we know it: A father, a family and an exceptional child.* New York: Pantheon Books.

Beck, M.N. (1999). *Expecting Adam: A true story of birth, rebirth and everyday magic.* New York: Times Books.

Buck, P. (1992). *The child who never grew.* Bethesda: Woodbine House.

Dorris, M. (1989). *The broken chord: A family's ongoing struggle with fetal alcohol syndrome.* New York: Harper and Row.

Featherstone, H. (1980). *A difference in the family: Living with a disabled child.* New York: Penguin Books.

Fowler, M. (1995). *Maybe you know my kid: Parent's guide to ADHD.* New York: Carol Publishing.

Gaul, G. M. (1993). *Giant steps: The story of one boy's struggle to walk.* New York: St. Martin's Press.

Gill, B. (1997). *Changed by a child: Companion notes for parents of a child with a disability.* New York: Doubleday.

Greenfeld, J. (1988). *A place for Noah.* San Diego: Harcourt Brace Jovanovich.

Hughes S. (1990). *Ryan: A mother's story of her hyperactive/tourette syndrome child.* Durante, CA: Hope Press.

Kaufman, S. Z. (1988). *Retarded isn't stupid, Mom!* Baltimore: Paul H. Brookes Publishing Co.

King Gerlach, E. (1999). *Just this side of normal: Glimpses into life with autism.* Eugene, Oregon: Four Leaf Press.

Kupfer, F. (1982). *Before and after Zachariah: A true story about a family and a different kind of courage.* Chicago: Academy Chicago Publishers.

Lelewer, N. (1994). *Something's not right: One family's struggle with learning disabilities.* Acton, MA: VanderWyk and Burnham.

Marsh, J.D. (1995). *From the heart: On being the mother of a child with special needs.* Bethesda: Woodbine House.

Maurice, C. (1993). *Let me hear your voice: A family's triumph over autism.* New York: Fawcett Columbine.

McAnaney, K.D. (1992). *I wish — Dreams and realities of parenting a special needs child.* Sacramento: United Cerebral Palsy Association of California.

McDonnell, J. T. (1993). *News from the border: A mother's memoir of her autistic son.* New York: Tichnor and Fields.

Meyer, D. J. (1995). *Uncommon fathers: Reflections on raising a child with a disability.* Bethesda: Woodbine House.

Miller, N. (Ed.) (1994). *Nobody's perfect: Living and growing with children who have special needs.* Baltimore: Paul H. Brookes Publishing Co.

Noble, V. (1993). *Down is up for Aaron Eagle: A mother's spiritual journey with down syndrome.* New York: HarperCollins.

Park, C. C. (1982). *The siege: The first eight years of an autistic child.* Boston: Little, Brown and Co.

Schaefer, N. (1997). *Yes! She knows she's here.* Toronto: Inclusion Press.

Schulze, C. (1993). *When snow turns to rain: One family's struggle to solve the riddle of autism.* Bethesda: Woodbine House.

Simons, R. (1985). *After the tears: Parents talk about raising a child with a disability.* San Diego: Harcourt, Brace and Co.

Spiegle, J. A. & R. A. van den Pol (Eds.) (1993). *Making changes: Family voices on living with disability.* Cambridge, MA: Brookline Books.

Sullivan, T. (1995). *Special parent, special child: Parents of children with disabilities share their trials, triumphs and hard-won wisdom.* New York: G. P. Putnam's Sons.

Weiss, E. (1989). *Mothers talk about learning disabilities: Personal feelings, practical advice.* New York: Prentice-Hall.

Zimmerman, S. (1998). *Grief dancers: A journey into the depths of the soul.* Golden, Colorado: Nemo Press.

ABOUT THE AUTHORS

Karen C. Mikus, MEd, PhD has been working with families of children with special needs and related professionals since 1970. She has a background in special education and is a practicing clinical psychologist. She has been a practitioner or an administrator in a variety of settings, including school systems, hospitals, and mental health organizations. Dr. Mikus serves on the faculty of the University of Michigan's post-masters Infant and Toddler Certificate Program in the School of Social Work where she teaches the course, *Working with Families of Children with Special Needs.* A frequent speaker and trainer for both parent and professional audiences, she also consults with school districts regarding the development and implementation of behavior management plans for students with challenges.

Janice Fialka, MSW, ACSW is married and the parent of two children, one of whom has developmental disabilities. She has worked in the field of adolescent health care for over twenty-five years as a social worker and administrator. Ms. Fialka is a national speaker and trainer on the topics of parent-professional partnerships and parenting a child with special needs. Ms. Fialka co-teaches a graduate social work class, *Social Work with Children with Disabilities and their Families,* at Wayne State University. She has published several of her poems and articles and has written a booklet, *It Matters: Lessons from My Son.*

HOW YOU MIGHT USE THIS BOOK

It is our hope that. . .

- as a **parent** of a child with special needs, you may find some of your own thoughts, feelings and experiences reflected in this book. This may bring some comfort, clarity or new ideas to your own situation. Most of us have experienced that "sigh of relief" when we've heard our inner voices reflected in someone else's story: "Oh! You've felt that too." We hope this sense of connection emerges for some of our readers.

- as a **professional** who works in the field of education, health care, mental health, advocacy, or parent support, you may identify with some of the concerns, experiences, and feelings discussed in this book. You may gain useful insights about or a heightened sensitivity to the challenges faced by parents, especially during the demanding experience of assessment and diagnosis. Your own struggles of working in this field may be validated as well.

- as a **trainer, university faculty member, or administrator** you may find this a useful resource to enhance your instruction, personnel preparation, supervision, and consultation. This book can be a valuable addition to partnership trainings at preservice and inservice levels, and at the undergraduate and graduate university levels. Using this book as a supplemental text in courses on assessment and intervention in the schools of education, social work, psychology, occupational and physical therapy, speech therapy, nursing, and medicine may bring the power of the personal voice into the classroom and training.

Other publications from Janice Fialka

It Matters: Lessons from my son

It Matters: Lessons from my son is a collection of poems and prose written by Janice Fialka, a social worker and mother of two children, one of whom has developmental disabilities. Her writings honestly describe the range of feelings and experiences of being a parent of a child with special needs. She writes about inclusion, use of labels, the power of support groups, and talking to siblings about special needs. She also includes suggestions for professionals. *It Matters: Lessons from my son* is full of honest emotions and insights for both parents and professionals.

ISBN 0-9791903-1-2

"It Matters is a wonderful book. Students in my class on the Psychology of Exceptional Children love it because the poems and essays draw them into the world of a family in a way that no textbook does. Student evaluations rate it as the most enjoyable and significant reading in the course."
Larry Lilliston, Ph.D.
Professor, Department of Psychology, Oakland University

Whose Life Is It Anyway?

How one teenager, her parents, and her teacher view the transition process for a young person with disabilities
Co-authored with Martha Mock and Jennifer Wagner Neugart in collaboration with the Waisman Center at the University of Wisconsin

This book provides insights into what youth, parents, and professionals experience as they plan for post-high school transition. It encourages the reader to think "outside the box."

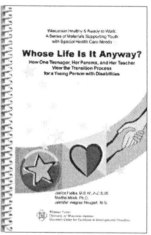

"The perspectives of the student, parent, and a teacher are a wonderful idea. Your book gives lots of insight into the transition process. I really like the length of the book and the discussion questions. I will use this book in my transition courses. What a creative work!"
Debra A. Neubert, Ph.D.
Department of Special Education, University of Maryland

From Puddles to Pride
A mother's poems about her son, his disability, and her family's transformation

On this CD, Janice reads three of her poems, accompanied by original piano music and a stunning PowerPoint presentation of photos and graphics. Two of the poems are from *It Matters: Lessons from my son.*

ISBN 0-9791903-2-0

This CD is simply beautiful. I have always enjoyed your writing, but with the slide show too, it is over the top!"
Mary Beth Doyle, Ph.D., St. Michael's College, Vermont

Through the Same Door
Inclusion Includes College

This inspiring film documents the new movement of fully inclusive education for students with cognitive disabilities on college campuses. As a high school student, Micah wanted the college experience and he got it. See how it is done, learn how it works, and witness how Micah's journey challenges us all to reexamine what we believe is possible. Winner of the 2006 TASH Image Award for the Positive Portrayal of People with Disabilities.

ISBN 0-9791903-0-4

"This is a very moving video about a young man with his family's support and vision, living life to its fullest with considerable challenges. Micah and his parents and teachers show the rest of us how possible and wonderful inclusion done with the proper supports can be. I watched this twice, soaking up the wisdom and warm feelings and getting a vision of a kinder, gentler world that values each and every person."
Robert Naseef, author, *Special Children, Challenged Parents:
The Struggles and Rewards of Raising a Child with a Disability*

To order any of these publications and to learn more about Janice's trainings:
www.danceofpartnership.com *or* **www.throughthesamedoor.com**
or call 248-546-4870